THE GREAT™
AMERICAN
HISTORY
QUIZ

America at War

THE GREAT™
AMERICAN
HISTORY
QUIZ

America at War

Series Created by
Abbe Raven and Dana Calderwood

Written by
**Charles Nordlander, Howard Blumenthal
and Dana Calderwood, with additional questions by
Bob Castillo, Megan Rickman and John Aherne**

WARNER BOOKS

An AOL Time Warner Company

Copyright ©2001 by A&E Television.
The History Channel, the "H" logo, and the Great American History Quiz are trademarks of A&E Television and are registered in the United States and other countries. All rights reserved.

Warner Books, Inc., 1271 Avenue of the Americas,
New York, NY 10020

Visit our Web site at www.twbookmark.com

For information on Time Warner Trade Publishing's
online publishing program, visit www.ipublish.com

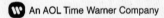 An AOL Time Warner Company

Printed in the United States of America

First Printing: December 2001
10 9 8 7 6 5 4 3 2 1

ISBN: 0-446-67838-4
LCCN: 2001095392

Cover design by Carolyn Lechter
Cover photographs by Corbis/Time Pix
Book design and text composition by Ralph Fowler

This edition of the quiz is called "America at War." This edition will explore the brave men and women who've fought to preserve our American way of life.

1 A fight sometimes breaks out over the simplest thing. A guy steps on your foot. Somebody cuts you off on the highway. Or the British come aboard your ships and take your sailors prisoner. And in 1812, the United States had had enough. The states had just won their freedom, yet Britain—which was at war with the French—was stopping U.S. ships enroute to France and forcing our sailors into the Royal Navy. But America wanted more than just maritime rights. What was another U.S. goal in the war?

(a) To gain possession of Canada

(b) To completely destroy the British navy

(c) To seize English colonies in the Caribbean

(d) To solidify relations with France

(a). There were a number of reasons the United States wanted Canada, among them land for expansion and for use as a bargaining chip with Britain. Not to mention, of course, the beer and hockey.

2 Today, Cuba is one of the biggest political thorns in America's side. So it's ironic that the seeds of the Spanish-American War were planted during Cuba's struggle for independence from Spain. U.S. intervention was aroused by sensational reports of Spain's brutal measures to subdue the Cuban rebels. The question is, where was the first battle in the Spanish-American War fought?

(a) Bay of Pigs

(b) San Juan Hill

(c) Manila Bay

(d) Havana

2

(c). A U.S. naval armada led by Commodore George Dewey entered Manila Bay, in the Philippines, on May 1, 1898, and destroyed the Spanish fleet.

And now, a few questions about the Korean War:

3 Who really remembers the details of the Korean War? It might be easier if we just put the war into *M*A*S*H* terms. Since Hawkeye and Major Burns were always squabbling, we'll call Syngman Rhee, the president of South Korea, Hawkeye. And Kim Il Sung, the leader of North Korea, is Major Burns. Plus, let's call Korea itself Hotlips.

Okay . . . in the late 1940s, both Hawkeye and Major Burns wanted a unified Hotlips. But the United States wanted a democratic Hotlips, and the Soviets wanted a Communist one. Using Burns and Hawkeye as puppets, the two superpowers set out to achieve their agendas. And on June 25, 1950, war began when the North invaded the South. How long after that did the United States become part of the conflict?

(a) The same day   **(c)** One month

(b) Three weeks   **(d)** Six months

A N S W E R

(a). U.S. troops in South Korea saw action from the very first day of the conflict. Wow, that sure was quick—but maybe Hotlips was worth it.

4 The UN forces fighting Communist North Korea were composed mainly of American and South Korean troops, though soldiers from fifteen other nations were also engaged. Nonetheless, the UN forces, led by General Douglas MacArthur, were having an extremely difficult time keeping the North Korean army at bay. In what is considered the single most brilliant strategic offensive of his military career, what kind of assault did General MacArthur lead on September 15, 1950, which proved to be a key element in forcing the Communist army to retreat back across the border?

(a) One of the first air strikes launched from carrier vessels at sea

(b) Surprise land assault modeled after the famous invasion of Hannibal over the Alps

(c) He faked a retreat with his center and crushed the enemy with his flanks

(d) An amphibious assault deep behind North Korean lines

4

(d). On September 15, 1950, MacArthur led a daring and highly effective amphibious assault on the port city of Inchon, deep behind enemy lines.

5 General Douglas MacArthur actively advocated an atomic attack on which country in 1950?

(a) Soviet Union

(b) North Korea

(c) China

(d) Vietnam

5

A N S W E R

(c). Fortunately, President Truman vehemently objected to this suggestion, and no more atom bombs were dropped after the horrors of Hiroshima and Nagasaki.

6 Why was General Douglas MacArthur removed as commander in Korea on April 11, 1951?

(a) General MacArthur was needed on Taiwan to help organize half a million Nationalist Chinese troops, which the U.S. government was galvanizing to overthrow the ruling Communist government of China

(b) General MacArthur was fired by President Truman after openly defying the president's plans for negotiating peace with North Korea

(c) After his tremendous contributions during two major wars, General MacArthur was ready to leave the battlefield, primed to become the popular presidential nominee in the upcoming 1952 election

6

A N S W E R

(b)

7 The Indian Wars began with the colonists on the Eastern seaboard and continued until almost the turn of the twentieth century, the gruesome battlefields moving westward with the advance of the frontier. Which of these is considered to be the last major battle of the Indian Wars?

(a) Tippecanoe

(b) Wounded Knee

(c) Sand Creek

(d) General Custer's Last Stand

ANSWER

(b). After the death of their great chief Sitting Bull, a band of Sioux, led by the warrior Big Foot, fled into the Badlands of southwestern Dakota. The Sioux were eventually surrounded by the U.S. 7th Cavalry, and 200 men, women, and children were massacred on the banks of Wounded Knee creek on December 29, 1890.

8 In 1887 the U.S. Congress passed a law granting individual landholdings to all Native Americans who would renounce their tribal holdings, a move designed to more easily absorb the Indians into the greater United States. The law was named after the acting chairman of the Committee on Indian Affairs. What was that man's name?

(a) H. L. Dawes

(b) W. M. Davis

(c) B. H. Day

(d) C. A. Debussy

8

(a) The Dawes Act was the work of Henry Laurens Dawes (1816–1903), a U.S. representative from Massachusetts. Just so you know, all these other men were more or less his contemporaries: William Morris Davis (1850–1934) was an American geologist, geographer, and teacher who founded the Association of American Geographers; Benjamin Henry Day (1810–1889) founded the *New York Sun* newspaper in 1833; and Claude Achille Debussy (1862–1918) was a French composer and exponent of musical expressionism.

Every man or woman who has ever answered the call to arms is a hero. But then there are a few who, for whatever reason, be it luck or destiny, have become legends for their heroism. Here are some questions about them.

9 After the Japanese attack on Pearl Harbor, America felt stunned and vulnerable. The military needed to strike back. So a risky mission was planned, in which B-25 bombers would attack Tokyo and six other cities. To carry it out, the hefty B-25s would have to take off from the shortened decks of an aircraft carrier—something they had rarely done before. Plus they carried scarcely enough fuel to fly to Japan and land safely in China. Who was chosen to lead the daring raid?

(a) Paul W. Tibbetts, Jr.

(b) Jimmy Doolittle

(c) Chuck Yeager

(d) William Mitchell

9

A N S W E R

(b) About four months after Pearl Harbor, Doolittle's Raiders took off from the U.S.S. *Hornet* and successfully bombed their targets in Japan. While the damage they inflicted was minor, Doolittle became a national hero, because the daring raid boosted America's sagging morale and gave hope to the struggle ahead.

10 During the Vietnam War, John McCain's bomber was shot down and both his arms and his right leg were shattered. He was taken prisoner and was told his injuries were too severe to treat. But when the Vietnamese realized he was the son of a U.S. admiral, they gave him just enough medical treatment to keep him alive as a propaganda tool. McCain survived his time in prisons like the infamous Hanoi Hilton thanks to his fellow prisoners and his own tenacity. How long was McCain held captive?

(a) Seven months

(b) A year and a half

(c) Almost four years

(d) Five and a half years

10

(d). His captors offered McCain early release, a move intended to sway his father's influence. But McCain refused, and he suffered torture and beatings before being forced to sign a phony admission of his "war crimes." He returned to the States in 1973, a hero and patriot.

11 By the end of World War I, Eddie Rickenbacker was America's most celebrated flying ace. But before the war, he wasn't a pilot at all—Rickenbacker was one of the nation's top racecar drivers. And when he entered the army, he became a driver for Colonel Billy Mitchell, the nation's leading advocate of military aviation. With Mitchell's help, Rickenbacker soon became a fighter pilot, and he downed more enemy planes than any other World War I American ace. How many enemy planes did Rickenbacker shoot down?

(a) 26

(b) 66

(c) 106

(d) 150

11

(a). Rickenbacker was awarded the Congressional Medal of Honor for once attacking seven German planes single-handedly. After the war, he wrote a book about his flying experiences and returned to car racing, eventually buying the Indianapolis Speedway.

Now, a few questions about the War of 1812 . . .

 When did the War of 1812 begin and end?

(a) February 1812 to August 1812

(b) 1812–1815; the war was named for the year it began

(c) 1810–1812; the war was named for the year it ended

(d) Though the war ended in 1811, the final peace treaty was not signed until 1812

12

(b). The fighting lasted for two and a half years and ended in early 1815.

13 What happened at the Battle of New Orleans?

(a) Jefferson's U.S. troops defeated a French army under Napoleon and won New Orleans for the United States

(b) General William Henry Harrison put down an uprising by Shawnee Indians

(c) General William Hull's U.S. forces, in the first real battle of the war, were roundly defeated by British-Canadian troops, with the result that Hull was later court-martialed and sentenced to death for cowardice

(d) General Andrew Jackson won the most significant American victory during the war in a battle fought two weeks after the war had ended

(d). The Treaty of Ghent was concluded on December 24, 1814, but remember, there was no Internet in the nineteenth century. Communication, especially across the Atlantic, was very slow, and official news of the peace agreement did not reach America until February!

Entertainment and war have always had an interesting relationship. Here are a couple of questions about some times when the two have mixed—literally.

14 It's a familiar story: Your favorite band is on tour, and the only way to get tickets is to pay a scalper. Well, during the Civil War, militia bands were in such demand that large sums of money were sometimes paid to get good musicians for a regiment. And what songs did these bands play? One smash hit of the Union army had original lyrics, but its tune was borrowed from another favorite anthem of the time, "John Brown's Body." What was the title of this Union army favorite?

(a) "Amazing Grace"

(b) "When Johnny Comes Marching Home"

(c) "Battle Hymn of the Republic"

(d) "When the Saints Go Marching In"

ANSWER

(c). Julia Ward Howe wrote the lyrics and sold them for five dollars. The song first appeared in 1862 and quickly became an anthem for Union troops.

15 From Bob Hope to Sheryl Crow, the USO has brought a touch of home to U.S. troops abroad for about sixty years. President Franklin D. Roosevelt helped launch the USO, along with General George C. Marshall and others. The idea was to improve the quality of life and morale in the military. At the height of World War II, the USO had over 3,000 clubs, and curtains rose 700 times a day at USO shows around the world. Since then, the organization has continued setting up recreation centers and drafting celebrities to entertain the troops. Which branch of government sponsors the USO?

(a) The State Department

(b) The Department of Defense

(c) The Department of the Interior

(d) None of the above

ANSWER

(d). Although chartered by Congress, the USO—which stands for United Service Organizations—is a nonprofit corporation. It relies mainly on public contributions and the efforts of its mostly volunteer staff.

16 True or False: The Navy WAVES, developed as an offshoot of the USO, was a group of women who flew to ships docked in foreign ports to sing, dance, and entertain navy men in active service.

16

False. The Navy WAVES (an acronym for Women Accepted for Volunteer Emergency Service) was founded during World War II—and the women weren't there simply to entertain the troops. Some 100,000 WAVES served in a wide variety of capacities, ranging from performing essential clerical duties to serving as instructors for male pilots-in-training. Several thousand WAVES also participated in the Korean War. The corps continued its separate existence until 1978.

17 What was the basis of Norman Mailer's 1967 book *Armies of the Night*, about the Vietnam War?

(a) The massacre at My Lai

(b) The mass exodus of conscientious objectors over the Canadian border

(c) The movement of small refugee enclaves through the forests of South Vietnam

(d) Two days of antiwar protests in Washington, D.C.

ANSWER

(d). Described as a new form of journalism combining the factual data and intimacy of a memoir with the perception of a novel, the book won a Pulitzer Prize.

18 Along with beat poet Alan Ginsburg, which of the following personalities did the U.S. government convict of conspiracy to aid the draft evasion movement?

(a) Dr. Seuss

(b) Dr. Spock

(c) Dr. Ruth

(d) Dr. Strangelove

18

A N S W E R

(b) Dr. Benjamin McLane Spock is most famous for his revolutionary *The Common Sense Book of Baby and Child Care,* but he was also an antiwar activist.

There are two defining struggles of the twentieth century. The Cold War: a battle between Russia and America, one side Red, the other Red, White, and Blue. And the Cola War: a beverage battle between Pepsi and Coke, one side brown, the other . . . brown. For each of the following events, you must decide whether it was part of the Cold War, the Cola War, or both.

19 In 1987, spending reaches $277 million. Does this represent the amount of money spent to wage the Cold War, the Cola War, or both?

A N S W E R

The Cola War. The U.S. defense budget actually far exceeded that amount. In 1987 Reagan's defense budget was approximately a thousand times as much—a whopping $282 billion.

20 Wisconsin Senator Joseph McCarthy spearheads a national campaign to defeat the enemy. Was this part of the Cold War, the Cola War, or both?

20

The Cold War. During the early 1950s McCarthy led the Senate permanent investigations subcommittee, which hunted down suspected Communists. "McCarthyism" ultimately became synonymous with "witch hunt" in America.

21 In 1985, former congresswoman and vice presidential candidate Geraldine Ferraro appears in controversial television ads. Was she a warrior of the Cold War, the Cola War, or both?

A N S W E R

The Cola War. Ferraro appeared in a hotly debated commercial for Diet Pepsi, causing some to question if she wasn't "selling out" her reputation.

22 An Atlanta scientist named John Pemberton develops the first version of an essential weapon to be used against the enemy. Was he an early soldier of the Cold War, the Cola War, or both?

ANSWER

The Cola War. In 1886 pharmacist John Pemberton invented the formula for Coca-Cola. By the 1890s, Coke was advertised with the catchy slogan "The ideal brain tonic."

23 American vice-president Richard Nixon and Soviet premier Nikita Khrushchev sit down together in Moscow in 1959 and share a beverage. Was this meeting an event in the Cold War, the Cola War, or both?

23

Both. At a Moscow trade fair, the two superpower leaders drank Pepsi together, and Pepsi would later win the exclusive right to sell its cola in the USSR.

Every human endeavor has its elite, a group that stands above the crowd. Sports has its Olympic medalists, music has its Grammy winners, and TV has its <u>Spin City</u> actors. But nowhere are the elite more important than in the military, where they can often make the difference between victory and defeat. Here are some questions about these elite forces.

24 Of all the elite forces in the U.S. military, rangers boast one of the longest histories. Men calling themselves rangers date back to the 1600s, when they scouted for Indians within a certain "range" of colonial settlements. During the Revolutionary War, it was a captain in a Connecticut rangers battalion who volunteered when Washington needed an officer to gather intelligence behind British lines. Disguised as a schoolmaster, this patriot collected information for a week before the British arrested and then executed him without a trial. Who was this ranger of the Continental Army?

(a) Patrick Henry   **(c)** Nathan Hale

(b) John Paul Jones   **(d)** Dr. Benjamin Church

24

(c). Nathan Hale was inducted into the Ranger Hall of Fame in 1993 for his outstanding service. As he prepared for his hanging, Hale spoke his immortal words "I only regret that I have but one life to lose for my country."

25 Long before there were Navy SEALs or Green Berets, the American military had another band of special forces— the Green Mountain Boys. This militia unit was organized in the 1760s at present-day Bennington, Vermont. Under the command of the legendary Ethan Allen, about 200 Green Mountain Boys led the way to capture Fort Ticonderoga from the redcoats in 1775. Why were the Green Mountain Boys originally formed?

(a) To serve as guides through Vermont's Green Mountains

(b) To hunt for moose

(c) To celebrate and preserve Irish culture

(d) To harass New York settlers

25

(d). The Green Mountain Boys sort of formed as Vermont's "UN-welcome Wagon." They often tarred and feathered New Yorkers who tried to claim Vermont's land as their own.

26 They fought against fascism, but were born of racism. That's the irony of the famed Tuskegee Airmen. The military, like most of America, was segregated during World War II. So Black pilot cadets were forced to train by themselves at the army air field in Tuskegee, Alabama. When these Black pilots entered the war, some even questioned their abilities because of their race. But by the end of the war, no one doubted the Tuskegee Airmen. Their four elite fighter squadrons won over 850 medals and compiled an incredible record while escorting bombers to their targets. Not a single bomber was ever lost under the fierce protection of the Tuskegee pilots. Who was their commander?

(a) Benjamin O. Davis Jr.

(b) John K. Cannon

(c) Booker T. Washington

(d) Colin L. Powell

A N S W E R

(a). Not only did Davis command the airmen, he also went on to become our nation's first black three-star general. Thanks in part to Davis and the airmen, President Truman signed an order in 1948 that ended military segregation.

27 The next series of questions is about military intelligence. Before you make any wildly hilarious jokes about "military intelligence" being an oxymoron, think about this: Military intelligence has often helped save lives and win wars. No oxymoron there.

No, "Paul Revere and the Liberty Boys" was not the name of a defunct 60s band. It was a defunct 70s band—the *1770*s, that is. That's when Paul Revere and other colonists created one of the first patriot intelligence networks. They spied on the British, served as couriers, and alerted patriot forces to redcoat troop movements. Which of the following locations was their secret meeting place?

(a) Old North Church

(b) Green Dragon Tavern

(c) Boston Common

(d) King's Chapel

27

A N S W E R

(b). Since the Liberty Boys met there a lot, it really wasn't much of secret. In fact, one of their "buddies" who hung out around the tavern was actually a British agent.

28 Morris "Moe" Berg burned the candle at both ends. When he wasn't practicing law at a big New York City law firm, he was spying for the U.S. government. During the early 1940s, Moe crisscrossed Europe on a top-secret mission to learn if Germany was close to creating an atom bomb. He helped German and Italian scientists defect to the United States. But amazingly, Moe Berg also had a third profession for which he became famous. What was it?

(a) Pro baseball player

(b) Physicist

(c) Television actor

(d) Novelist

28

A N S W E R

(a) Moe Berg was a catcher on five major league baseball teams over a fifteen-year career. Hey, some kids dream of being a ballplayer, others dream of being a secret agent. Moe Berg got to do both.

29 During World War II, the United States developed a code based on the language of a Native American tribe. The code was incredibly complex and difficult to break, because only a handful of people outside the tribe knew the language. What Native American tribe did the U.S. Marines enlist to develop this code?

(a) Shawnee

(b) Apache

(c) Navajo

(d) Cheyenne

29

(c). Roughly 400 Navajos served as code talkers during World War II, and the code was never broken.

30 Nothing demonstrates the horrors of war better than the personal stories of the way it affects families and touches lives. The next category is about some of these tragedies.

Captain D. P Conyngham, a Northern officer, told this tale shortly after the Civil War. "I had a Sergeant Driscoll," he said, "a brave man and one of the best shots." Under fire, Driscoll vowed to take down a young Southern officer, so he raised his rifle and shot him. Combing the field later, they found the body of the fallen Southerner. "The frantic grief of Driscoll was harrowing to witness," Conyngham recalled. He watched Driscoll collapse over the young man, who whispered this dying word: "Father." In the fury of war, Sergeant Driscoll had killed his own son. This tragedy occurred at Malvern Hill, during the Seven Days' Battles. Which Southern city were Union troops trying to capture?

(a) Richmond   **(c)** Atlanta

(b) Charleston   **(d)** Savannah

30

(a). During the Seven Days' Battles, the North tried unsuccessfully to capture Richmond, Virginia, the capital of the Confederacy. The fighting at Malvern Hill was so ferocious and bloody that one Confederate general remarked, "It was not war—it was murder."

31 The five Sullivan brothers of Waterloo, Iowa, made a special request when they enlisted in the navy during World War II: They asked to serve together. The navy granted their wish, and they were soon aboard the USS *Juneau*. But then that wish turned into a horrifying tragedy, when a torpedo slammed into the *Juneau*. Four Sullivan brothers went down with the ship, while the fifth clung desperately to a raft for days—only to drop from sheer exhaustion and die in the shark-infested waters. What did the government do to honor the brothers?

(a) Passed a law to prevent siblings from serving together

(b) Created the Sullivan Medal for Bravery

(c) Erected a monument to them in Washington, D.C.

(d) Named two ships after them

31

(d). The navy named two destroyers after the Sullivans, the second one after the first ship was decommissioned. There's a common myth that a law was enacted to prevent siblings from serving together, but no such law exists.

32 When the Gulf War broke out, Americans turned to CNN for the latest from Baghdad. But during World War II, we relied on journalist Ernie Pyle. Pyle was the eye-witness for the common man. He wrote simple, intimate words that told Americans of the horror and savagery that their boys were facing overseas. As a fan of Ernie's once put it, "He wouldn't be on a balcony looking down . . . he'd be in a foxhole looking up." And so it was that Ernie Pyle would die. While under attack in a ditch, he raised his head to look out, and machine-gun fire pierced his temple. Which honor did Pyle receive after his death?

(a) Pulitzer prize

(b) Medal of Freedom

(c) Purple Heart

32

(c). Pyle was honored with a Purple Heart, an award rarely given to a civilian. As General Omar Bradley once said: "My men always fought better when Ernie was around."

You've heard the expression "War is not healthy for children and other living things," right? Well, sometimes it's the other living things that do the fighting. Here's what we mean.

33 In the midst of the Revolutionary War, a lost dog strayed into General Washington's army camp. The Continental soldiers soon discovered that the dog belonged to their sworn enemy, British General William Howe. Howe's name was engraved right on the dog's collar. What did George Washington do with the dog?

(a) Exchanged it for POWs

(b) Returned it under a flag of truce

(c) Kept it as an army messenger dog

(d) Executed it by firing squad

33

A N S W E R

(b). Washington himself owned many dogs for fox hunting, and he surely sympathized with General Howe's loss. With the dog safely returned, Washington and his troops could get back to the job of trying to kill the dog's owner and his men.

34 Did Flipper and Shamu work as covert agents for the U.S. Navy? Well, not exactly. But the navy's secret Marine Mammal Program has trained beluga whales, sea lions, and dolphins to carry out underwater surveillance. A dolphin's sensitive sonar, for example, is superb at detecting underwater mines and possible enemy swimmers. In which war were dolphins used for military operations?

(a) World War II

(b) The Persian Gulf War

(c) None

(d) The Vietnam War

34

(d). Dolphins were used during the Vietnam War, where their patrols ended underwater sabotage at Cam Ranh Bay. Rumors have also circulated for years about a "swimmer nullification program," in which dolphins are trained to kill enemy swimmers—but the navy has always denied its existence.

There was a time when advanced weaponry consisted of a rock and a spear. But, sadly, ever since men have lived in caves, we've been looking for better ways to wage war. On that note, here are some questions about weapons that changed war forever.

35 The now distinctive sound of rapid-fire shooting was first heard in 1862. That is when Dr. Richard Gatling demonstrated his new invention, the Gatling gun. His six-barrel model fired up to 200 rounds per minute—by far the fastest bullet-firing killing machine at the time. What was Dr. Gatling's motivation for inventing the gun?

(a) To reduce the number of lives lost in battle

(b) To advance America's military capabilities

(c) To build an improved weapon for hunters

(d) To sell the patent to Germany

35

(a). Gatling figured that if he could create a device that did the "work" of many soldiers, fewer would die. Fewer on our side, at any rate. He also believed that if war became even more gruesome, governments would try to find a more peaceful alternative.

36 On August 6, 1945, the history of humanity changed forever. The U.S. bomber *Enola Gay* dropped the first atom bomb ever used in warfare. It is estimated that 70,000 or more were killed instantly at Hiroshima, and the death toll at least doubled in the aftermath. Three days later, the United States dropped a second atom bomb on the city of Nagasaki. Use of the bomb has remained a hotly debated issue, but it did bring a decisive end to the war with Japan. After the bombings of Hiroshima and Nagasaki, how many atom bombs did the United States have left in its arsenal?

(a) Zero

(b) One

(c) Three

(d) Twelve

36

A N S W E R

(a). There were none, although more bombs could have been produced in a short period of time. As it happened, the power of the Hiroshima-type bomb would soon pale in comparison to a new generation of even deadlier weapons of mass destruction.

37 During the Persian Gulf conflict, one type of missile ushered in a new age in warfare. It was so accurate, you could launch one from Shea Stadium and hit a fifteen-foot-wide target all the way in Atlanta! This missile was capable of "seeing" its target and then matching what it saw to an image stored in its computer. Plus, pilots weren't put at risk to launch or guide this weapon to its target. What missile is being described?

(a) The Tomahawk

(b) The Patriot

(c) The SCUD

(d) The HAAD

37

A N S W E R

(a). The latest models of the Tomahawk Cruise missile can travel distances up to 1,000 miles and have an added feature: GPS, a global positioning system, which gives them almost as much control as some major league pitchers.

And now, a few questions about the Spanish-American War...

38 Which of these methods was successfully used to garner American sympathy and support for Cuba's war of independence against the island's ruling country, Spain?

(a) Radio broadcasts by President McKinley known as "fireside chats"

(b) The highly dramatic air-drop of tens of thousands of pro-rebel pamphlets, which littered the state of Florida for weeks and alerted hundreds to the Cuban plight under Spanish rule

(c) Tabloid newspapers, aka the "yellow press"

(d) A beautiful Cuban activist ironically called "Spanish Rose," who toured the states raising American awareness of the Cuban plight

(c). Our modern tabloid newspapers find their roots in the yellow press, which sold thousands of copies by printing melodramatic stories of the violence and terror occurring in Cuba's fight for sovereignty. News from Cuba filtered through these sources tended to be skewed and provocative, but managed to gain the Cuban rebels many American sympathizers. And we hope you didn't fall for answer **(b)**: Remember that the Wright brothers had their first successful flight only in 1903, and aircraft were nowhere near sophisticated enough for airdrops.

39 The names wars are given follow two paths: There is the common name, which usually includes the names of the nations fighting, the territory that was fought over or in, or the years during which the battles were waged—i.e., the War of 1812 or the Persian Gulf War. Another name remembers the war for what it was meant to be or resulted in, such as calling World War I the "Great War," or the Korean War the "Forgotten War." What is the colloquial name for the Spanish-American War?

(a) The Bloody War

(b) The Soldier's War

(c) The Splendid Little War

(d) The Franciscan War

39

(c). It was "little" because the fighting only lasted three months, although we can all agree that no war is "splendid."

40 When Spain declared war on America on April 24, 1898, what action did the U.S. Congress immediately take?

(a) Sent 10,000 additional troops into the capital city of Madrid, under the command of General George Dewey

(b) Sent a U.S. squadron led by Admiral George Dewey into Manila, where the resident Spanish fleet was thoroughly defeated within a few hours

(c) Called for a draft of all young American men between the ages of sixteen and nineteen

(d) Declared war retroactively on Spain, dating from April 21

ANSWER

(d). On April 25 Congress declared that a state of war had existed since April 21, when diplomatic relations were broken off.

41 The First Volunteer Cavalry was composed of Ivy Leaguers and cowboys both. Who was this "cowboy cavalry's" most famous member?

(a) Theodore Roosevelt

(b) George Dewey

(c) Nelson A. Miles

(d) William McKinley

41

A N S W E R

(a). Not only was Teddy Roosevelt largely responsible for organizing this unique force, but he also resigned his post as assistant secretary to the navy in order to engage in the fighting. Leonard Wood served as colonel of the regiment, while Roosevelt acted as lieutenant colonel and an active soldier.

42 With what name did the press christen the First Volunteer Cavalry?

(a) Teddy's Gang

(b) Salvation Army

(c) El Matadors

(d) Rough Riders

ANSWER

(d). Roosevelt had even coined the term "roughrider"—meaning a cowboy—in an article for *Century Magazine* in 1888.

43 Out of 5,462 American lives lost during the years of the Spanish-American War, how many of them were actual battle casualties?

(a) 379

(b) 1,420

(c) 5,400

(d) 5,462

(a). Only 379 soldiers were killed in combat. The other 5,083 men died of yellow fever, malaria, and other diseases—not to mention poisoning from tainted meat given to soldiers for their rations.

44 By the treaty that ended the war in 1898 the United States acquired Guam, the Philippines, and Puerto Rico. What other territory was annexed that same year and completed the "stepping stones" desired for creation of a new American Pacific empire?

(a) The Caroline Islands

(b) The Hawaiian Islands

(c) Midway Island

(d) Bikini Island

44

ANSWER

(b). The U.S. minister to Hawaii, John L. Stevens, had wanted to annex the Hawaiian Islands as early as 1893, after Queen Liliuokalani was deposed, but President Grover Cleveland had refused. The islands were annexed under President McKinley in 1898, and Sanford B. Dole was made president of the new Hawaiian republic.

45 What other territory, now a very popular vacation spot for college students especially, did America obtain from Spain in 1819?

(a) Mexico

(b) Cuba

(c) Cancun

(d) Florida

45

(d). After years of diplomatic wrangling, the United States acquired Florida under the Adams-Onis Treaty, in exchange for America's assumption of $5 million in damage claims by U.S. citizens against Spain.

When you hear the phrase "war propaganda," you probably think of the other side: the bad guy goose-stepping to an evil drum. But as the saying goes, what's good for the propa goose is good for the propa ganda . . .

46 Remember the *Maine*? Newspapermen like Joseph Pulitzer and William Randolph Hearst made sure no one would ever forget it. When the U.S. battleship *Maine* blew up in Cuba's Havana harbor, these two men accused Spain of sabotage in outraged editorials and stories. Their brand of journalistic propaganda was filled with inaccuracies and even outright lies—but it sure sold plenty of papers. In 1976, a team of experts reinvestigated the fate of the *Maine*. What did they conclude was the cause of the explosion?

(a) A mine planted in the bay

(b) An accidental explosion

(c) Cannon shots fired from shore

(d) A suicide mission funded by Spanish landowners

46

A N S W E R

(b). The investigation concluded that the *Maine* was destroyed by an accidental explosion aboardship. But the team's findings were almost eighty years too late. The belief that the Spanish had sabotaged the *Maine* was the spark that ignited the Spanish-American War.

47 Her name was Iva Toguri, an American citizen of Japanese descent, whose birthday was the Fourth of July. At her parents' request, Iva went to Japan to care for a sick aunt. But after the bombing of Pearl Harbor, she was stuck there, unable to return home. During her stay, the Japanese forced Iva to work as a radio announcer on a show scripted by Allied POWs. They were supposed to write propaganda to undermine U.S. morale. In truth, the POWs and Iva outwitted the Japanese with shows that had a lighthearted, upbeat tone. What happened to Iva Toguri at the end of the war? Was she:

(a) Invited to the White House

(b) Given her own radio show

(c) Shot while touring a POW camp

(d) Convicted of treason

47

A N S W E R

(d). In an atmosphere of wartime hysteria, Iva was convicted of treason, jailed for over eight years, and branded in the headlines as "Tokyo Rose." This terrible injustice can never truly be undone—but in 1977, President Gerald Ford finally pardoned Iva Toguri on his last day in office.

48 Nowadays, carpooling is encouraged as a good idea. But it was serious business in America during World War II. A rubber shortage meant that tires had to be rationed—and the federal government rationed gasoline too, as a way to cut auto use and conserve rubber. There were even posters from the era that criticized people who drove alone. See if you can complete the slogan on this World War II carpooling poster: "When you ride alone . . ."

(a) " . . . you burn rubber."

(b) " . . . you hurt the war effort."

(c) " . . . you kill a soldier."

(d) " . . . you ride with Hitler."

48

ANSWER

(d). The complete, and very subtle, slogan was "When you ride alone, you ride with Hitler!" Imagine what a backseat driver that guy could be.

Now let's turn our attention to World War I for a few questions about America's role in that conflict.

49 Which president was met with wild applause and overwhelming support after delivering a powerful war request to congress, to which he responded: "My message today was a message of death for our young men. How strange it seems to applaud that."

(a) Woodrow Wilson

(b) William McKinley

(c) Franklin Roosevelt

(d) Grover Cleveland

49

A N S W E R

(a). In 1917, three years after the First World War began, Wilson gave a speech to Congress declaring that America must join the fighting in Europe to defend liberty and create a new stability. President Wilson recognized that while the reason a nation goes to war may be righteous and noble, the realities of a generation of men going to war are necessarily tragic.

50 In 1917 the Zimmerman Telegram was intercepted by the British Secret Service and used to sway President Woodrow Wilson to fully engage American troops in Europe's war. What country was German foreign minister Arthur Zimmerman attempting to entice to fight against the Allies, promising in return to award that government the states of Texas, Arizona, and New Mexico?

(a) Canada

(b) Russia

(c) Switzerland

(d) Mexico

50

ANSWER

(d). Once this explosive memo was brought to light, President Wilson recognized how very close to home the war had almost come and was pushed further toward action.

You know, from time to time, everybody makes mistakes, even our military leaders. Which leads us to our next America at War category: "Lack of Military Intelligence."

51 Let's see. When it comes to mistakes a soldier can make in battle, there's losing your helmet, missing your target, and of course, accidentally shooting your own general in the back. That last mishap actually happened in the Civil War at the battle of Chancellorsville. General Stonewall Jackson was shot by a sentry in his own army and died later from complications. While Jackson himself was buried in Lexington, Virginia, there's another part of him that was buried elsewhere. What was it?

(a) His Confederate uniform

(b) His left arm

(c) His heart

(d) His beloved horse

51

(b). His left arm had to be amputated as a result of his wounds. It is buried fifteen miles west of Fredericksburg, Virginia, at the Ellwood plantation. Robert E. Lee recognized the terrible blow to the Confederacy when he commented that while Jackson had lost his left arm he himself had lost his right.

52 The year is 1988. Tensions are high in the Persian Gulf. U.S. ships patrol the waters, protecting Kuwaiti oil tankers from Iranian air attacks. Suddenly, a blip on radar. The call goes out, "Friend or foe?" The response is misunderstood, missiles are locked and launched, and then the horrible truth is revealed: An Iranian passenger jet has been shot down by mistake, killing 290 people onboard. What American ship was responsible for this tragic failure of military intelligence?

(a) The USS *Stark*

(b) The USS *Vincennes*

(c) The USS *Enterprise*

(d) The USS *Nimitz*

52

ANSWER

(b). The crew of the *Vincennes* had mistaken the passenger jet for an Iranian F-14 fighter. According to U.S. authorities, the men were operating under more liberal rules of engagement, which were established after thirty-seven sailors had been killed by an Iraqi fighter jet.

53 If you're planning on bombing a country, there are several things you'll need: a bomb, a few planes, and an accurate map so that you'll know what you're bombing. Otherwise you could do what the United States did on May 7, 1999, when we accidentally bombed the Chinese embassy in Belgrade because of inaccurate maps and poor intelligence. The bombing occurred as part of a conflict in the Balkan region. Where was it being fought?

(a) Bosnia

(b) Kosovo

(c) Albania

(d) Macedonia

53

ANSWER

(b). Chinese students in Beijing protested the bombing by throwing rocks at the U.S. embassy, trapping the U.S. ambassador inside.

And now some questions about the Second World War...

54 Everyone knows *Casablanca* as the famous movie starring Humphrey Bogart and Ingrid Bergman. But what important event actually took place in Casablanca, beyond the beginning of "a beautiful friendship"?

(a) An Allied invasion that signified the beginning of the end for the fascists

(b) A 1943 conference where Franklin Roosevelt and Winston Churchill mapped out the invasion of Europe

(c) Where Mussolini was tried and executed by firing squad

(d) A meeting between the USSR and Allied leaders that resulted in the Soviet Union secretly promising aid against Japan

54

(b). But do you know the questions that led to the other answer choices? You should! It's history! The invasion on the beaches at Normandy was considered to be the strike that initiated the end of the war and the defeat of the Axis nations. Mussolini, after living the last year of his life as the puppet leader of a German fascist enclave in northern Italy, was taken to Milan, where he was tried and executed, and his body was hung in the public square. The meeting at which the USSR promised their help against Japan was called the Yalta Conference. Now you know!

55 The amendment that granted the U.S. government the exclusive right to build a naval base at Pearl Harbor was ratified in what year?

(a) 1778

(b) 1887

(c) 1891

(d) 1937

55

(b). But the other dates are all important in Hawaii's history too: It was in 1778 that British explorers led by Captain James Cook first "discovered" the islands, though they had been well populated since c. 750 B.C.E. In 1891 the beloved Queen Liliukalani was deposed and a provisional republic was established under U.S. supervision. And statehood for the Hawaiian Islands was proposed in 1937, though ultimately rejected by Congress.

56 How many American lives are estimated to have been lost during the Japanese attack on Pearl Harbor alone?

(a) 750

(b) 2,000

(c) 4,000

(d) 10,000

A N S W E R

(b). In addition to the loss of life, 19 ships, including 8 battleships, were sunk or disabled, and 177 aircraft were destroyed on the ground.

57 On the same day they made their attack on Pearl Harbor, Japanese forces also launched offensives against numerous other sites. Which of the following was NOT one of the Japanese targets?

(a) Guam

(b) The Philippine Islands

(c) Hong Kong

(d) Bikini Island

57

A N S W E R

(d). Within twenty-four hours of the December 7 attack on Pearl Harbor, Japan had also launched attacks against Malaya, Wake Island, and Midway Island.

58 During the latter years of the war, many factories used for industrial goods during peacetime were converted to function as military suppliers for the war effort. In light of this, someone commented that America had become the "arsenal of democracy." Who said that?

(a) Franklin Roosevelt

(b) Boss Tweed

(c) Harry S Truman

(d) Winston Churchill

58

(a). Not only were factories converted to produce different goods, but the workforce within the factories changed radically as well. With all the able-bodied men off to war, it was American women who kept the factories running and our boys supplied.

59 In 1943 Americans were being forced to cut back on most luxuries and many necessities due to rationing. For instance, how many pairs of leather shoes do you think Americans were permitted to own per year?

(a) Three

(b) Ten

(c) Fifteen

(d) As many as they wanted to, since shoes have never been rationed in America

59

(a). Three pairs of leather shoes a year does not sound like many, but only a decade earlier, during the Depression years, thousands of families had no shoes at all.

60 Which of the following key figures of World War II was NOT made aware that the scientists of the Manhattan Project were building the atom bomb until 1945, the same year it was dropped?

(a) Douglas MacArthur

(b) Franklin Roosevelt

(c) Winston Churchill

(d) Harry Truman

60

(d). While it was ultimately Truman's decision to drop the A-bomb, during his years as vice president he had been kept in the dark about the work at Los Alamos. Once he was informed, the new president initially resisted General MacArthur's urging to launch an atomic attack.

61 In 1939 President Roosevelt received a letter warning that European scientists were making great advances toward creating an atomic weapon. The letter encouraged Roosevelt to establish a U.S. program to develop atomic capabilities in order that no power in Europe—where such research programs were already established—would be able to hold the world hostage with a weapon of mass destruction. Partially in response to this, though not until 1943, Roosevelt established the Manhattan Project and the atom bomb was built. Which famous figure wrote this galvanizing letter?

(a) Winston Churchill

(b) Albert Einstein

(c) Future German prime minister Helmut Kohl

(d) Charles DeGaulle

61

(b). Albert Einstein warned Roosevelt that the only way to prevent any country from using such extreme power was for America to have equal power—a system of checks and balances. The atom bomb was successfully built by the scientists of the Manhattan Project at the Los Alamos lab in New Mexico in 1945. Only a few months after the first test explosion, almost 100,000 people were killed by the atomic warheads dropped on Japan. Though his intentions had been good, Einstein later regretted writing the letter to Roosevelt, feeling a sense of complicity in the bloody destruction he had helped make possible.

62 When Franklin Delano Roosevelt died only months after winning an unprecedented third term in office, which of the Axis "enemy" countries issued a sympathetic message in respect for his death?

(a) Japan

(b) Germany

(c) Italy

(d) China

62

A N S W E R

(a). Even between enemies, the loss of a great leader can be felt deeply.

63

What does the "D" in D-Day stand for?

(a) Day of Destruction, signifying the date of a highly destructive attack, such as Pearl Harbor

(b) Day of Defeat, signifying the date of the last decisive battle in a war, which forces the enemy to surrender

(c) Day of Designation, signifying the date when a military operation is planned— i.e., August 6 was D-Day for the bombing of Hiroshima

(d) Dogtag Day, the day when a soldier first receives his ID tags

ANSWER

(c). There were actually many such "D-Day"s, but June 6, 1944, remains the most memorable.

64 Operation Overlord was one of the most famous and pivotal events of the Second World War and was led by future president General Dwight D. Eisenhower. What was this operation?

(a) Allied troops invaded the beaches of Normandy

(b) U.S. aircraft bombed Nagasaki and Hiroshima

(c) U.S. invasion of the Philippine island of Leyte, which within one year allowed America to establish practical control over the Philippines

64

ANSWER

(a). The invasion of Normandy.

65 The Allied invasion of Normandy is generally considered to be the beginning of the end for Hitler. How long after the invasion did Germany actually surrender?

(a) Eighteen days

(b) Four months

(c) Eleven months

(d) Eighteen months

65

(c). Germany accepted an unconditional surrender the night of May 7, 1945—eleven months and a day after the invasion.

66 To what does the "Battle of the Bulge" refer?

(a) A successful surprise attack by the German army on Allied troops in Luxembourg and Belgium, at a time when the Germans were generally considered to have been generally defeated

(b) The title, coined jokingly by the media, for the open animosity that existed between President Harry Truman and General Douglas MacArthur

(c) The personal battle being waged by Winston Churchill in an effort to keep his formidable size in check

66

ANSWER

(a). It was called the Battle of the Bulge because the Germans forced the Allies to retreat in that sector, which created a "bulge" in the lines.

War is full of pivotal moments that forever change the course of events. Try to answer these questions about some decisive battles that turned the tide of war.

67 You can usually tell where battles were fought because they're often named for the location. And in June of 1775, an important battle took place in the Revolutionary War on a hill that's now part of Boston. Where was this historic battle fought?

(a) Breed's Hill

(b) Blue Hill

(c) Bunker Hill

(d) Beacon Hill

67

ANSWER

(a). Breed's Hill is the place where the Battle of Bunker Hill was actually fought. The two hills are close by, and their names were sometimes switched on old maps. That may explain how such a famous battle could be misnamed, but the truth is that no one really knows for sure.

68 It may be the most famous American image from World War II: U.S. marines raising the flag during the pivotal battle for Iwo Jima. In the course of a month-long struggle, nearly 30,000 soldiers died for control of a volcanic island that measures about eight square miles. The Japanese were dug in to defend Iwo Jima, the marines were intent on taking it. But what was the strategic importance of Iwo Jima to the American war effort? Was it:

(a) The first U.S. victory in the Pacific

(b) A safe harbor for submarines

(c) It had no strategic importance

(d) A good base for U.S. planes

68

(d). Because of its location, Iwo Jima was a good aircraft base. By the way, that famous "raising of the flag" on Iwo Jima was actually a do-over! The first flag raised by the marines was too small to be seen by our troops.

69 Although scarcely a shot was fired, the Cuban Missile Crisis may have been the most pivotal battle of the Cold War. In 1962, Soviet leader Nikita Khrushchev began an effort to base nuclear missiles in Cuba aimed at the United States. President Kennedy threatened to invade Cuba if the missiles were not removed. And Khrushchev warned that nuclear war could be the inevitable result of such a confrontation. For thirteen days, the world stood at the brink of World War III. The standoff ended when a secret compromise was reached. What promise did Kennedy deliver to Khrushchev?

(a) To send a $400 million aid package to Cuba

(b) To release over 1,500 Cuban POWs

(c) To halt a planned assassination of Castro

(d) To remove U.S. missiles from Turkey

69

(d). When Kennedy secretly offered to remove nuclear missiles in Turkey that were aimed at the Soviet Union, the Soviets agreed to withdraw their missiles in Cuba, thus ending the missile crisis. But the crisis of getting your hands on a Cuban cigar in the States still continues.

While most recent wars involving America have been fought on foreign soil, that doesn't mean the impact wasn't felt here at home. This is clearly evidenced by our next series of questions, titled "On the Home Front."

70 On the home front during World War I, anything or anyone connected to Germany was suspect. And America tried to rid itself completely of German culture. So the town of Germany, Indiana, was renamed Pershing. The Kaiserhof Hotel in Chicago became the Atlantic. And if your name was Kirschberger, you might have changed it to—say—Smith. This de-Germanizing even extended to dogs! So here's your question: In 1917, what did Americans call dachshunds?

(a) Star-Spangled Spaniels

(b) Freedom Dogs

(c) Patriot Pups

(d) Liberty Pups

70

(d). And dachshunds weren't alone in getting new, liberty-oriented names. Sauerkraut became liberty cabbage and the hamburger was renamed the liberty sandwich.

71 Long before Howard Stern or Rush Limbaugh, there was another wildly popular radio host: President Franklin D. Roosevelt with his fireside chats. FDR's radio talks helped lift the nation's spirits during the great Depression and the war years. His very first chat convinced Americans to put one billion dollars back in the troubled banks. And in another talk, Roosevelt sat down with an atlas to educate citizens about the geography of World War II. He was patient, personal, and congenial. How often, on average, did FDR deliver his fireside chats?

(a) Two to three times a week

(b) Once a month

(c) Two to three times a month

(d) Two to three times a year

ANSWER

(d). FDR delivered a total of only twenty-seven chats during his four terms in office. But that was enough. As the historian David McCullough once said, "When he came on the radio, you listened whether you liked him or not."

72 Back on the home front during World War II, Uncle Sam asked Americans to get out their hoes and fight the enemy without ever leaving their yards. You see, the war effort put a real strain on the nation's supply of produce. So Americans rallied by growing their own fruits and vegetables in so-called victory gardens, which sprang up throughout the United States. The question is: What percentage of the nation's vegetables did victory gardens provide?

(a) Less than 1 percent

(b) 15 percent

(c) 25 percent

(d) 40 percent

72

A N S W E R

(d). By 1943, victory gardens were producing an astonishing 40 percent of America's fresh vegetables. And no wonder—by that same year, 20 million victory gardens had been planted.

And now, on to the Vietnam War . . .

73 The division of Vietnam into "north" and "south" was never intended to be permanent. The country was divided in 1954, as part of a cease-fire agreement between the French and Vietnamese. After two years, Vietnam was supposed to be reunified through free, national elections. But in 1956, South Vietnam's leader, Ngo Dinh Diem, refused to hold the elections and honor the agreement. What did the United States do in response?

(a) Secretly planned to assassinate Diem

(b) Backed his refusal to hold elections

(c) Censured Diem in the United Nations

(d) Remained neutral

73

A N S W E R

(b). Fearing the spread of Communism in Asia, the United States supported Diem's refusal to hold elections and provided economic and military aid for his government. It was a fateful decision on the long, twisted path that would lead the country into the Vietnam War.

74 What unconditional pardon did President Jimmy Carter pass on January 21, 1976, one day after his inauguration?

(a) The unconditional pardon for 10,000 men who had evaded the draft, most of whom had trekked north to Canada

(b) The unconditional pardon for former president Richard Nixon, who had resigned from his presidential office in disgrace just a year earlier

(c) The unconditional pardon for Lieutenant William L. Calley, commander of the soldiers responsible for the "dark and bloody" massacre at My Lai, in which 560 innocent Vietnamese elders, women, and children were gunned down

74

(a). The draft evaders were pardoned by President Carter. Lieutenant Calley was actually pardoned by Richard Nixon, while Richard Nixon was pardoned by Gerald Ford.

75 The war in Vietnam and the years of military buildup that preceded it touched on the terms of five American presidents—Eisenhower, Kennedy, Johnson, Nixon, and Ford—spanned sixteen years, and claimed approximately how many American lives?

(a) 60,000

(b) 40,000

(c) 80,000

(d) 1 million

75

(a). 60,000 lives is a tremendous number to lose, and this figure does not include the tens of thousands of Vietnamese casualties. But compare that number to World War I, "the war to end all wars": 120,000 U.S. soldiers died and another 200,000 were left wounded, despite America's only very brief engagement at the end of war. The countries that bore the brunt of the fighting fared even worse: 10 million soldiers died on the battlefields and another 20 million died from disease, famine, and other war-related causes. Almost an entire generation of men from Russia, Britain, France, and Germany was lost.

76 How many tons of bombs—not including the tons of Agent Orange and other highly destructive chemical defoliants—were dropped on Vietnam during the years of the war?

(a) 3 million tons

(b) 5 million tons

(c) 7 million tons

(d) 15 million tons

76

A N S W E R

(c). 7 million tons.

From Vietnam, we travel to the Middle East for a few questions on the Gulf War . . .

 In order to justify his invasion of the small neighboring country of Kuwait, what did Saddam Hussein accuse Kuwait of?

(a) A Kuwaiti military buildup that seemed to indicate a forthcoming attack on Iraq by Kuwait: Saddam was merely preempting a Kuwaiti invasion

(b) Overproduction of oil and theft of oil from the Iraqi Rumailia oil field

(c) Having a religious majority that was incongruous with the Muslim majority of Iraq and the surrounding areas of Arabic countries

(d) Being in cahoots with Iran in an attempt to dominate the world oil market

A N S W E R

(b)

78 Who was serving as secretary of defense during Operation Desert Storm?

(a) Dick Cheney

(b) Colin Powell

(c) Stormin' Norman Schwarzkopf

(d) James Webb

78

(a). Now vice president, Dick Cheney was then serving as secretary of defense.

79 What gesture of support to U.S. troops did President George Bush Sr. make in November of 1990?

(a) The president personally made sure that each soldier serving in the desert had a proper Thanksgiving meal, complete with cranberry sauce and stuffing

(b) The president made sure that there was also a vegetarian meal offered, for those infantrymen who preferred it, complete with tempe turkey and soy stuffing

(c) The president actually ventured to the Middle East to spend Thanksgiving in the desert with the American soldiers

79

ANSWER

(c)

80 On August 7, 1990, Operation Desert Shield was launched and the Persian Gulf War officially began. What was this operation "shielding"?

(a) The safety of Kuwaiti citizens and the security of hospitals, banks, government centers, and other civic properties important to the function of Kuwaiti society

(b) The oil fields of Saudi Arabia, which the United States feared were next to be invaded by Saddam Hussein and his army

(c) Operation Desert Shield was the configuration flight pattern for U.S. military jets that flew low and close together in a successful effort to blanket Iraqi targets with bombs

80

A N S W E R

(b)

81 On January 18, 1991, coalition forces from thirty-two UN member nations launched Operation Desert Storm. Under whose command were these UN forces?

(a) Marlin Fitzwater

(b) Robert McFarlane

(c) Norman Schwarzkopf

(d) Colin Powell

81

(c). "Stormin' Norman" was in command.

82 In which war did the "Black Shoe Army" fight?

(a) War of 1812

(b) World War II

(c) Vietnam

(d) Persian Gulf War

82

(c). During the Vietnam War, for the first time ever, U.S. Army soldiers were required to wear black shoes with their uniforms, instead of the traditional brown. The soldiers resented this changeover greatly, as black shoes were traditional to the navy and air force.

What book about America at War could be complete without a section on the Civil War, the one war where we actually fought each other. Here is a series of questions about the War between the States. For the following famous Civil War battles, name the side that won the battle:

83

First Battle of Bull Run?

83

A N S W E R

The Confederacy.

84 Shiloh?

84

A N S W E R

The Union.

85

Second Bull Run?

85

A N S W E R

The Confederacy again.

86 Siege of Fredericksburg?

86

A N S W E R

That was a Union victory.

87 Gettysburg?

87

A N S W E R

The Union.

88 Speaking of Gettysburg, who could forget Lincoln's famous address at Gettysburg cemetery? What most people have forgotten, if they knew it in the first place, is that Lincoln wasn't the only orator delivering a speech that day. Who was the other orator who had to share the stage with Lincoln?

(a) Jefferson Davis

(b) Robert E. Lee

(c) John C. Breckinridge

(d) Edward Everett

88

(d). The principal speaker at the ceremonies dedicating the military burial ground was Edward Everett, a famous orator of his day and the former governor of Massachusetts. While Lincoln's memorable speech only lasted two minutes, Everett's oration went on a bit longer than that: It clocked in at over two hours.

89 True or false: The Civil War cost America the most casualties?

ANSWER

Sadly, the answer is **true.** According to *The World Almanac* statistics, approximately 360,000 Union soldiers and 135,000 Confederates were killed during the Civil War, making it the bloodiest war in American history.

"War is hell," but we have to admit that America's wars have produced some memorable utterances. For the next couple of questions, we'll give you a famous quote. You have to identify the war with which it is associated. And for extra credit, try to identify the speaker.

 Let's start with an easy one: When a famous general said that "war is hell," what particular war was he talking about?

90

A N S W E R

Civil War. When he addressed a group of veterans in 1880 William Tecumseh Sherman was actually condemning war in general, but he must have had in mind his experiences during the Civil War.

91

"Damn the torpedoes! Full speed ahead!"

91

Civil War. A "torpedo" in those days was a floating mine, and some two hundred of them protected the entrance to Mobile Bay, in Alabama. When Admiral David Farragut plowed his way into the harbor with a Union fleet in August 1864, it was certainly a heroic action but not as foolhardy as his instructions would seem: His gunboats were guided by pilots who knew where the mines were planted and could steer around them.

"Nuts!"

92

ANSWER

World War II. In January of 1945, during the Battle of the Bulge, German Panzer units surrounded the men of the 101st Airborne Division in the city of Bastogne. When called upon to surrender, General Anthony "Old Crock" Macauliffe reportedly delivered this famous one-word reply. Inspired by their commander's gruffness, the paratroopers managed to hold off the German advance until they were relieved.

93 "Don't shoot until you see the whites of their eyes!"

93

Revolutionary War. Tradition has it that this instruction was given to American militiamen during the Battle of Bunker Hill. Various patriot leaders have been given credit for this sensible advice, among them General Israel Putnam and Colonel William Prescott.

94

"I have not yet begun to fight!"

94

Revolutionary War. During its epic sea battle with the British frigate *Serapis*, the *Bonhomme Richard* took a tremendous beating and actually began to sink. Despite his losses, American commander John Paul Jones refused to strike his colors, and it was the British captain who eventually surrendered.

95 "We have met the enemy and they are ours!"

A N S W E R

War of 1812. With this laconic dispatch Captain Oliver Hazard Perry announced that he had wrested control of the Great Lakes from the British. Ironically, the naval battle of Lake Erie on September 10, 1813, both began and ended with a memorable quote: The signal pennant that Hazard hoisted from the mast of his flagship to open the battle bore the motto "Don't Give Up the Ship!"

And let's finish off the book where it all began: The American Revolution . . .

96 The Declaration of Independence got the old revolutionary ball rolling. How many grievances against the king of England were listed in the Declaration?

(a) Ten

(b) Twelve

(c) Twenty-seven

(d) Fifty

96

ANSWER

(c). There were twenty-seven grievances against the king of England listed in Thomas Jefferson's Declaration of Independence.

97 Another early act that got us on the road to revolution was the Boston Tea Party, in which fifty people, poorly disguised as Mohawk Indians, boarded three ships in Boston Harbor and began dumping tea out right and left. What was the name of the political group that went on this decaffeinated rampage?

(a) The Sons of Liberty

(b) The Daughters of Liberty

(c) The Sons of the Pioneers

(d) The Sons of the Revolution

97

(a). The Sons of Liberty, which claimed Samuel Adams as one of their members, instigated the Boston Tea Party.

98 This revolutionary war hero had more career ups and downs than John Travolta: After leading the American forces to victory at the Battle of Saratoga in 1777, he took part in a misguided attempt to take control of the army from George Washington later that year. When he was given command of the army in the south, he made another bad career move by being routed in a major battle in South Carolina and losing command of his forces. He redeemed himself, however, after the war and was eventually reinstated as the army's second-ranking officer. Who was this erratic revolutionary hero?

(a) Nathaniel Greene

(b) Horatio Gates

(c) John Paul Jones

(d) Israel Putnam

ANSWER

(b). Horatio Gates.

99 Not all of the colonists were so eager to break away from England. Approximately what percent of the population remained faithful to the British Crown during the Revolution?

(a) About 10 percent

(b) About 33 percent

(c) About 50 percent

(d) About 75 percent

99

(b). Historians estimate that about a third of the population was actually rooting for the British during the Revolutionary War.

Which came first? The Battle at Lexington or the Boston Massacre? The Boston Tea Party or the Declaration of Independence? So many battles, so many milestones on the road to independence. It's sometimes difficult to keep them all straight. Well, let's see if you can . . .

 Put the following events in the order in which they occurred:

Boston Massacre

Declaratory Act

Stamp Act

Townshend Acts

100

A N S W E R

The **Stamp Act,** which placed hefty tariffs on almost every kind of printed matter from legal documents to playing cards, was enacted in 1765. The **Declaratory Act,** which was passed in 1766, reasserted the right of the British Parliament to impose laws and collect taxes from the colonies. The **Townshend Acts,** a series of import taxes on glass, lead, paints, paper, and tea, took effect in 1767. The **Boston Tea Party,** the last of these revolutionary measures, took place in 1774.

101 And in what order did these seminal revolutionary moments take place?

The Battle of Bunker Hill

The signing of the Declaration of Independence

The Battles at Lexington and Concord

The capture of Fort Ticonderoga from the British

A N S W E R

The **Battles at Lexington and Concord** took place on April 19, 1775. Ethan Allen and Benedict Arnold **captured Fort Ticonderoga** on May 10 of that year. The **Battle of Bunker Hill** took place on Breed's Hill over a month later, on June 17. And the **Declaration of Independence** wasn't signed until July 4, 1776.